500
REALLY USEFUL
SPANISH
WORDS
AND PHRASES

Written and edited by
Carol Watson and Janet De Saulles

Illustrated by
Shelagh McNicholas

— Contents —

This book was created by Zigzag Publishing Ltd, The Barn, Randolph's Farm, Brighton Road, Hurstpierpoint, BN6 9EL

The consultant, Maria Dolores Le Fanu, was born and brought up in Spain. She has a degree in Spanish and the History of Art from the University of London, and teaches Spanish and English in England.

Pronunciation guide: Rosa Ellis

Editor: Janet De Saulles
Managing Editor: Nicola Wright
Designers: Suzie Hooper, Jonathan Skelton
Design Manager: Kate Buxton
Series concept: Tony Potter

Colour separations by RCS Graphics Ltd, Leeds
Printed in Italy

First published in the USA in 1994 by Hippocrene Books Inc., 171 Madison Avenue, New York, NY10016

Copyright © 1993 Zigzag Publishing Ltd

ISBN 0 7808 0262 8

10 9 8 7 6 5 4 3 2 1

About this book

In this book you will find out how to speak Spanish. You will meet the González family who will show you what to say in many different situations. Here they are to introduce themselves.

¡Hola! Somos el Señor y la Señora González.
(Olla! Somoss el Senyor ee la Senyora Gonzalez.)
Hello! We are Señor and Señora González.

¡Hola! Soy Miguel.
(Olla! Soy Miggel.)
Hello! I'm Miguel.

¡Hola! Soy Carmen.
(Olla! Soy Carmen.)
Hello! I'm Carmen.

Everything the González family says is written in Spanish and English. There is also a guide to pronouncing the Spanish words.

¡Hola! Soy Carmen. —— these are the Spanish words
(Olla! Soy Carmen.) —— this shows you how to pronounce the Spanish
Hello! I'm Carmen.
—— this is what it means in English

How to speak Spanish

These notes will help you to use the pronunciation guide:

Say 'a' like the 'a' in 'bad'. Say 'o' like the 'o' in 'top'.
Say 'e' like the 'e' in 'bed'. Say 'oo' like the 'oo' in 'good'.
Say 'ay' like the 'ay' in 'say'. Say 'ch' like the 'ch' in 'church'.
Say 'ee' like the 'ee' in 'feet'. Say 'cee' like the word 'see'.

- 'B' is used for the Spanish 'v'.
- 'Ny' is used in the guide to make the sound of the Spanish 'ñ'.
- 'H' is used for the Spanish 'j' and is pronounced like the 'h' in 'hole'.

¿Question marks?

When there is a question or exclamation mark at the end of a sentence, the Spanish also put an upside-down question or exclamation mark at the beginning of the sentence.

Speaking to people

When you speak to a close friend or a relative, you use **tú**. If there is more than one friend or relative, you use **vosotros** (or **vosotras** if the group is female only). When you speak to somebody you do not know very well, you use **usted**. If there is more than one person you use **ustedes**.

Accents

In general, the second to last syllable of a Spanish word is stressed. When a different syllable is stressed, it is marked by an accent.

Masculine and feminine words

In Spanish, some words are masculine and some are feminine. **La** in front of a word means that it is is feminine and **el** usually means that it is masculine. For example, 'house' is feminine in Spanish - '**la** casa', while 'book' is masculine - '**el** libro'.

When the word is plural, for example, books or houses, then it has **las** or **los** in front of it ('**las** casas' and '**los** libros'). **Las** is the feminine plural and **los** is the masculine plural.

Meeting people

In the evenings, the González family often goes to the town center for a walk. When Hispanic people meet somebody that they do not know very well, they use the polite form of Spanish. Children also use this polite form when they speak to people older than themselves.

To say 'How are you?' in polite Spanish you can use '¿Cómo está?'. If you are speaking to more than one person you can say '¿Cómo están?'.

Buenas noches, Señor Sánchez. ¿Cómo está?
(Bwennas nochess, Senyor Sanchez. Como esta?)
Good evening, Señor Sanchez. How are you?

Muy bien, gracias.
(Mwee bee-en, grasyas.)
Very well, thank you.

When you meet somebody you know well, you can say '¿Cómo estás?'. If you are talking to more than one friend you can say '¿Cómo estáis?'.

¡Hola! ¿Cómo estás?
(Olla! Como estas?)
Hello! How are you?

Bien, gracias.
(Bee-en, grasyas.)
Fine, thank you.

Carmen and Miguel meet two children they have seen once before.

¡Hola! ¿Cómo os llamáis?
(Olla. Como os yamayis?)
Hello. What are you called?

Me llamo Francisco.
(May yamo Frasisco.)
I'm called Francisco.

Nos llamamos Carmen y Miguel.
(Nos yamamos Carmen ee Miggel.)
We're called Carmen and Miguel.

Tengo diez años.
(Tengo deeyez anyos.)
I'm ten years old.

¡Vámonos! ¡Hasta luego!
(Bamonos! Asta lwego!)
Let's go! See you later!

¿Nos vemos aquí mañana?
(Nos bemos akee manyanna?)
Shall we meet here tomorrow?

¡Yo también!
(Yo tambee-en!)
Me too!

De acuerdo. Hasta mañana.
(Day akwerdo. Asta manyanna.)
OK. See you tomorrow.

Meeting people words

buenas tardes
(bwennas tardes)
good afternoon/
good evening

buenos días
(bwennos dee-as)
good morning

adiós
(addyoss)
goodbye

¿y tú?
(ee too?)
and you?

bastante bien
(bastantay bee-en)
quite well

Making friends

On their way home from school, Carmen and Miguel talk to an English boy and girl who started at their school that day. They talk about their families and where they live.

Family words

la familia
(la fameelya)
family

los padres
(los padress)
parents

el padre
(el padray)
father

el abuelo
(el abwelo)
grandfather

el tío
(el tee-o)
uncle

la tía
(la tee-a)
aunt

la madre
(la madray)
mother

la abuela
(la abwela)
grandmother

la hermana
(la ermana)
sister

el hermano
(el ermano)
brother

el primo
(el preemo)
cousin (male)

la prima
(la preema)
cousin (female)

el hijo
(el i-ho)
son

la hija
(la i-ha)
daughter

Finding the way

Señora González has taken her children out for the day. Before they go home they decide to have something to eat at a nearby café.

Por favor señora, ¿hay un café por aquí?
(Por fabbor senyora, eye oon caffay por akee?)
Excuse me madam, is there a café near here?

No.
(No.)
No.

¿Está lejos?
(Esta layhos?)
Is it far?

Por allí y gire a la izquierda.
(Por ayee ee heeray ah la izkeeyerda.)
Over there and turn left.

la cabina telefónica
(la cabeena telefonnika)
telephone booth

la gasolinera
(la gasolinerra)
gas station

los servicios
(los serbeeceeyos)
toilets

el buzón
(el boozon)
mailbox

Direction words

todo recto
(toddo recto)
straight on

frente a
(frentay ah)
opposite

al lado de
(al laddo day)
next to

a la derecha
(ah la deretcha)
on the right

a la izquierda
(ah la izkeeyerda)
on the left

After their meal, they ask a man the way to the station.

On the way home, Carmen gets lost. Her mother tries to find her.

¿Dónde está la estación, por favor?
(Donday esta la estacyon, por fabbor?)
Where is the station, please?

Está a la derecha.
(Esta ah la deretcha.)
It's on the right.

Me he perdido.
(May ay perdeedo.)
I am lost.

¡No encuentro a mí hija!
(No encwentro ah mee i-ha!)
I can't find my daughter!

el aeropuerto
(el aeropwerto)
airport

el hospital
(el ospital)
hospital

la comisaría
(la comisareeya)
police station

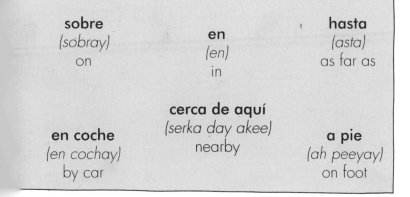

sobre
(sobray)
on

en
(en)
in

hasta
(asta)
as far as

cerca de aquí
(serka day akee)
nearby

en coche
(en cochay)
by car

a pie
(ah peeyay)
on foot

la iglesia
(la iglessya)
church

Staying in a hotel or house

The Spanish often have the whole month of August as holiday. During this month the González family likes to go to different parts of Spain. This year they are staying in a hotel for the first week, and in a friend's house for the second.

Nos gustaría reservar una habitación para una semana.
(Nos goostareeya reserbar oona abitaceeyon parra oona semanna.)
We would like to book a room for one week.

Sí señores. ¿Qué desean ustedes?
(See senyores. Kay desayan oostedes?)
Yes, sir and madam. What would you like?

Una habitación doble con baño, por favor.
(Oona abitaceeyon dobblay con banyo, por fabbor.)
A double room with a bathroom, please.

¡Me gusta este hotel!
(May goosta estay otel!)
I like this hotel!

la almohada
(la almwadda)
pillow

la sábana
(la sabbanna)
sheet

el mozo
(el mozo)
porter

el balcón
(el balkon)
balcony

la cama
(la camma)
bed

la casa
(la casa)
house

arriba
(areeba)
upstairs

el dormitorio
(el dormitorreeyo)
bedroom

el cuarto de baño
(el cwarto day banyo)
bathroom

la butaca
(la bootacca)
armchair

la sala de estar
(la salla day estar)
living room

el televisor
(el telebissor)
television set

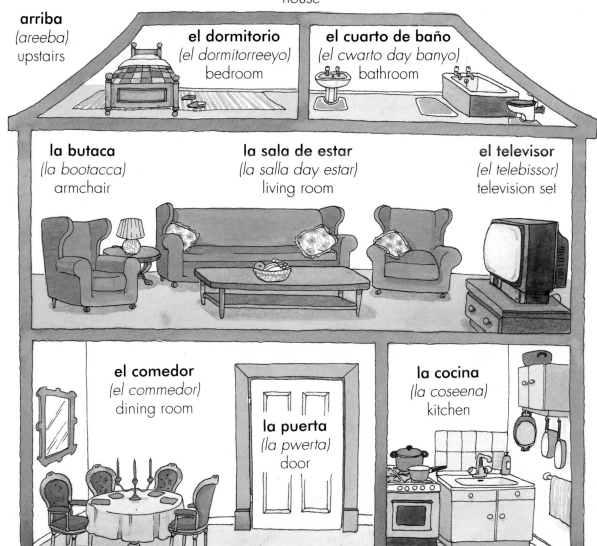

el comedor
(el commedor)
dining room

la puerta
(la pwerta)
door

la cocina
(la coseena)
kitchen

las contraventanas
(las contrabentannas)
shutters

la ventana
(la bentanna)
window

la mesa
(la messa)
table

la silla
(la seeya)
chair

11

Camping

The González family is spending the last week of August on a campsite. Most Spanish campsites provide electricity, so that the campers can watch television or enjoy themselves as they would at home.

Por favor, ¿pueden hacer un poco menos de ruido?
(Por fabbor, pwedden aser oon poco mennos day rooeedo?)
Please could you make a little less noise?

Some more useful camping words and phrases

agua potable
(agwa potahblay)
drinking water

reservado para remolques
(reserbahdo parra remolkays)
recreational vehicles only

agua no potable
(agwa no potahblay)
non-drinking water

la tela impermeable
(la tella impermayabblay)
groundsheet

el camping
(el camping)
campsite

la tienda de campaña
(la teeyenda day campanya)
tent

el palo de la tienda
(el pallo day la teeyenda)
tent pole

el camping gas
(el camping gas)
camping gas

la estaca de la tienda
(la estacca day la teeyenda)
tent peg

el saco de dormir
(el sacco day dormeer)
sleeping bag

las duchas
(las doochas)
showers

el mazo
(el maso)
mallet

el colchón neumático
(el colchon newmattico)
airbed

¿Dónde están los servicios, por favor?
(Donday estan los serbeeceeyos, por fabbor?)
Where are the toilets, please?

Lo siento, ni idea.
(Lo seeyento, nee iday-ah.)
I'm sorry, I've no idea.

Están al lado de la tienda del camping.
(Estan al laddo day la teeyenda del camping.)
They are next to the campsite shop.

Going shopping

In most parts of Spain, the shops are open
from 9 in the morning until 2 in the afternoon. They open
again at 5 and close for the day at 8 in the evening.

¿Puedo ayudarle?
(Pweddo ayoodahlay?)
Can I help you?

Querría dos panes, por favor.
(Kerreeya doss pannes, por fabbor.)
I would like two loaves, please.

Food words

la leche
(la lechay)
milk

la mantequilla
(la mantekeeya)
butter

el yogurt
(el yogoort)
yoghurt

el huevo
(el webo)
egg

la patata
(la patatta)
potato

la col
(la coll)
cabbage

el tomate
(el tomattay)
tomato

la naranja
(la naranha)
orange

la manzana
(la manzanna)
apple

la carne
(la carnay)
meat

el pollo
(el pollo)
chicken

el azúcar
(el asoocar)
sugar

la mermelada
(la mermeladda)
jam

la carnicería
(la carnisereeya)
butcher's shop

el supermercado
(el supermercaddo)
supermarket

la panadería
(la pannadereeya)
bakery

Although the Spanish like to go to their local shops, supermarkets are being used more and more.

¿Cuánto es?
(Cwanto ess?)
How much is it?

Dos mil pesetas.
(Doss meel pessettas.)
Two thousand pesetas.

¿Desea algo más?
(Desaya algo mass?)
Would you like anything else?

Un kilo de tomates, por favor.
(Oon keelo day tomattess, por fabbor.)
A kilo of tomatoes, please.

la farmacia
(la farmaceeya)
pharmacy

la librería
(la librereeya)
bookshop

la tienda de ultramarinos
(la teeyenda day ultramareenos)
grocery shop

The post office and bank

Carmen and Miguel are at their local post office (correos y telégrafos).

¿Cuánto cuesta enviar este paquete?
(Cwanto cwesta enbeeyar estay pakettay?)
How much is it to send this parcel?

¿A dónde?
(Ah donday?)
Where to?

A Inglaterra.
(Ah Inglaterra.)
To England.

If you want to post letters abroad, look for a letter-box marked 'extranjero'.

Now Carmen is telephoning a friend. When the Spanish answer the telephone they say 'dígame'.

¡Dígame! ¿Quién habla?
(Deegamay! Keeyen abla?)
Hello! Who's speaking?

Soy Carmen. ¿Puedo hablar con Teresa, por favor?
(Soy Carmen. Pweddo ablah con Teressa por fabbor?)
It's Carmen. May I speak to Teresa please?

el dinero
(el dinerro)
money

el banco
(el banco)
bank

la moneda
(la monedda)
coin

la carta
(la carta)
letter

la tarjeta postal
(la tarhetta postal)
postcard

Post office and bank words

correos y telégrafos
(corrayos ee telaygrafos)
post office

por avión
(por abyon)
airmail

número de teléfono
(noomerro day telayfono)
telephone number

Te llamo más tarde.
(Tay yammo mass tarday.)
I'll call you back later.

enviar
(enbeeyar)
to send

extranjero
(extranherro)
foreign

el tipo de cambio
(el teepo day cambyo)
exchange rate

Señor González has gone to the bank to change some Spanish pesetas into English pounds and pence.

¿A cuánto está la libra?
(Ah cwanto esta la leebra?)
How many pesetas are there to the pound?

el sello
(el seyo)
stamp

el billete
(el beeyettay)
note

el paquete
(el pakettay)
parcel

el teléfono
(el telayfono)
telephone

la tarjeta de crédito
(la tarhetta day creditto)
credit card

Eating out

The González family often has Sunday lunch at a friendly local restaurant.

Un vaso de vino tinto, por favor.
(Oon basso day beeno tinto, por fabbor.)
A glass of red wine, please.

Quiero una limonada.
(Keeyerro oona limmonadda.)
I'd like a lemonade.

¿Qué más desean?
(Kay mass dessayan?)
What else would you like?

Un agua mineral, por favor.
(Oon agwa minneral, por fabbor.)
Mineral water, please.

¿Te gusta el helado de fresa?
(Tay goosta el elahdo day fraysa?)
Do you like strawberry ice cream?

No, prefiero el helado de chocolate.
(No, prefeeayro el elahdo day chocolatay.)
No, I prefer chocolate ice cream.

el vaso
(el basso)
glass

el menú
(el menoo)
menu

la ensalada
(la ensaladda)
salad

el filete
(el filettay)
steak

las patatas fritas
(las patattas freetass)
French fries

el pescado
(el peskaddo)
fish

la paella
(la pie-ayah)
paella

el camarero
(el cammarerro)
waiter

La cuenta, por favor.
(La cwenta, por fabbor.)
The bill, please.

¡Aquí lo tiene!
(Akee lo teeyennay!)
Here it is!

¡Buen provecho!
(Bwen probbecho!)
Enjoy your meal!

¿Está bueno?
(Esta bwenno?)
Is it good?

Sí. Está muy rico.
(See. Esta mwee reeko.)
Yes. It's very tasty.

¿Me puedes pasar la sal?
(May pweddess passar la sal?)
Could you pass me the salt?

¡Tengo hambre!
(Tengo ambray!)
I'm hungry!

¡Tengo sed!
(Tengo sed!)
I'm thirsty!

la tortilla de patatas
(la torteeya day patattas)
Spanish omelette

una taza de café
(oona taza day caffay)
a cup of coffee

una jarra de agua
(oona harra day agwa)
a jug of water

19

Visiting places

Spain is famous for its sunshine and sandy beaches. As well as going to the seaside, the González family also likes to visit old Spanish castles and small white-washed villages.

Useful visiting words

el partido de fútbol
(el parteedo day footbol)
soccer match

el parque de atracciones
(el parkay day attrakseeyonness)
fairground

el centro turístico
(el thentro turistico)
tourist centre

el palacio
(el palathee-o)
palace

el castillo
(el casteeyo)
castle

la película
(la paylikoola)
film

las cuevas
(las cwebbas)
caves

el teatro
(el tayattro)
theater

el circo
(el seerko)
circus

la obra de teatro
(la obbra day tayattro)
play

el museo
(el moossayo)
museum

el cine
(el seenay)
cinema

Games and sports

la gimnasia
(la gymnassiya)
gymnastics

el fútbol
(el footbol)
soccer

el patinaje
(el patteenahay)
skating

la natación
(la nattaceeyon)
swimming

el cricket
(el cricket)
cricket

la equitación
(la ekeetaceeyon)
riding

el windsurf
(el windsoorf)
windsurfing

Carmen and Miguel have met up with some of their friends in the local park.

¿A qué estáis jugando?
(Ah kay estayiss hoogando?)
What are you playing?

A béisbol.
(Ah basebol.)
Baseball.

¿Cómo se juega? ¿Es difícil?
(Como say hwegga? Ess difeeseel?)
How do you play? Is it difficult?

No. Es fácil.
(No. Ess faseel.)
No. It's easy.

¿Me dejáis jugar?
(May dayhayiss hoogar?)
Can I play?

¡Claro! Necesitamos dieciocho personas.
(Klaroh! Nesesitamos deeyeseeocho personas.)
Of course! We need eighteen people.

el juego del escondite
(el hweggo del eskondeetay)
hide and seek

el ping-pong
(el ping-pong)
ping-pong

la pesca
(la peska)
fishing

practicar el remo
(practicah el remo)
rowing

el ciclismo
(el seekleesmo)
cycling

¿Dónde está la pelota?
(Donday esta la pelota?)
Where is the ball?

¡Está aquí!
(Esta akee!)
It's here!

¡Te toca a ti!
(Tay tocca ah tee!)
Your turn!

el poste
(el postay)
post

¡Tengo sueño!
(Tengo swenyo!)
I'm tired!

el palo
(el pallo)
bat

el judo
(el hoodo)
judo

el esquí
(el eskee)
skiing

el footing
(el footing)
jogging

el tenis
(el tennis)
tennis

el golf
(el golf)
golf

el baloncesto
(el balonsesto)
basketball

Accidents and illnesses

The González family keeps all its emergency telephone numbers near the telephone. In Spain there are different numbers for police, ambulance and fire emergencies.

¡Socorro!
(Socorro!)
Help!

¡Fuego!
(Fweggo!)
Fire!

Accident words

¡Cuidado!
(Cweedaddo!)
Watch out!

el coche de la policía
(el cochay day la poliseeya)
police car

la urgencia
(la urgenseeya)
emergency

¡Han entrado a robar en mi habitación!
(An entraddo ah robah en mee abitaceeyon!)
My room has been burgled!

la herida
(la ereeda)
injury

¡Me han robado el bolso!
(May an robaddo el bolso!)
My handbag has been stolen!

la ambulancia
(la ambulanseeya)
ambulance

¡Vengan pronto!
(Bengan pronto!)
Come quickly!

¡Me han robado el billetero!
(May an robaddo el beeyeterro!)
My wallet has been stolen!

24

Me duele la cabbeza.
(May dwellay la cabbeza.)
I have a headache.

el termómetro
(el termommetro)
thermometer

Me duele el estómago.
(May dwellay el estommago.)
I have a stomach ache.

el médico
(el meddico)
doctor

la pastilla
(la pasteeya)
pill

la receta
(la resetta)
prescription

la venda
(la benda)
bandage

la enfermera
(la enfermerra)
nurse

Illness words

Tengo una erupción.
(Tengo oona erroopceeyon.)
I have a rash.

la tirita
(la tireeta)
adhesive bandage

¡Tengo fiebre!
(Tengo feeyebbray!)
I have a temperature!

Tengo dolor de muelas.
(Tengo dollor day mwellas.)
I have a toothache.

el dentista
(el denteesta)
dentist

Tengo algo en el ojo.
(Tengo algo en el o-ho.)
I have something in my eye.

25

Travelling

**The González family is driving to the railway station.
They are all meeting some friends from Madrid.**

On the way, the family stops the car for some more gas.

¿Dónde está la estación de servicio más cercana?
(Donday esta la estaceeyon day serbeeceeyo mass thercanna?)
Where is the nearest gas station?

Todo recto.
(Toddo recto.)
Straight on.

← la taquilla	la consigna ↑	la sala de espera →
(la takeeya)	*(la consin ya)*	*(la salla day esperra)*
ticket office	left luggage office	waiting room

¿Dónde está la taquilla?
(Donday esta la takeeya?)
Where is the ticket office?

¿A qué hora llega el tren de Madrid?
(Ah kay orra yega el tren day Madrid?)
At what time does the train from Madrid arrive?

A las once.
(Ah las onsay.)
At eleven o'clock.

Detrás de usted.
(Detras day oosted.)
Behind you.

You can find out more about how to say the
time in Spanish by looking at page 28.

Later, the friends go into the town center by themselves.

¿Dónde está la parada del autobús para el centro ciudad?
(Donday esta la paradda del owtobooss parra el sentro ceeoodad?)
Where is the bus stop for the town center?

Está aquí.
(Esta akee.)
It's here.

bajarse
(baharsay)
to get off

el pasajero
(el passaherro)
passenger

subirse
(soobeersay)
to get on

Travelling words

coger el autobús
(cohair el owtobooss)
to catch the bus

el billete de ida y vuelta
(el beeyettay day eeda ee bwelta)
return ticket

el billete
(el beeyettay)
ticket

el mapa
(el mappa)
map

el camión
(el camyon)
truck

dirección única
(dirrekceeyon oonika)
one way

la calle
(la kaiyay)
street

el coche
(el cochay)
car

coger el tren
(cohair el tren)
to catch the train

reservar un asiento
(reserbar oon asseeyento)
to reserve a seat

el autocar
(el owtocar)
coach

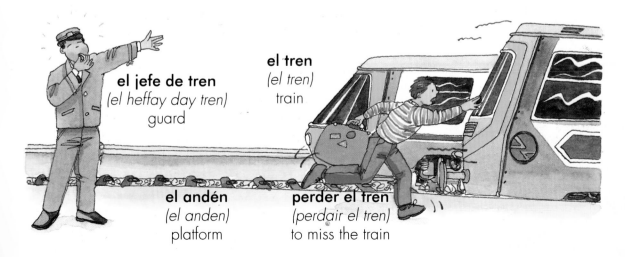

el jefe de tren
(el heffay day tren)
guard

el tren
(el tren)
train

el andén
(el anden)
platform

perder el tren
(perdair el tren)
to miss the train

More useful words

Time

The Spanish do not use the words 'past' or 'to' when they tell the time. Instead, they use the words 'and' (y), or 'less' (menos).

¿Qué hora es, por favor?
(Kay orra ess, por fabbor?)
What time is it, please?

Son las cinco.
(Son las ceenko.)
It is five o'clock.

Son las cinco y diez.
(Son las ceenko ee deeyez.)
It is ten past five.

Son las cinco y cuarto.
(Son las ceenko ee cwarto.)
It is quarter past five.

Son las cinco y media.
(Son las ceenko ee medya.)
It is half past five.

Son las seis menos cuarto.
(Son las seys mennos cwarto.)
It is quarter to six.

Es mediodía.
(Ess medyodee-a.)
It is midday.

Es medianoche.
(Ess medyanochay.)
It is midnight.

Times of the day

la tarde
(la tarday)
afternoon

la noche
(la nochay)
night

la mañana
(la manyanna)
morning

la tarde
(la tarday)
evening (early)

la noche
(la nochay)
evening (late)

The months of the year and days of the week

enero
(enerro)
January

febrero
(febrerro)
February

marzo
(marzo)
March

abril
(abreel)
April

mayo
(mayo)
May

junio
(hooneeyo)
June

The Spanish do not use capital letters at the beginning of the names of the months or the days of the week.

lunes	**martes**	**miércoles**
(looness)	*(martess)*	*(meeyercolles)*
Monday	Tuesday	Wednesday
	jueves	**viernes**
	(hwebbess)	*(beeyernes)*
	Thursday	Friday
	sábado	**domingo**
	(sabbaddo)	*(domingo)*
	Saturday	Sunday

The seasons

la primavera
(la preemaberra)
spring

el verano
(el beranno)
summer

el otoño
(el ottonyo)
autumn

el invierno
(el inbeeyerno)
winter

julio
(hooleeyo)
July

agosto
(agosto)
August

septiembre
(septyembray)
September

octubre
(octoobray)
October

noviembre
(nobbyembray)
November

diciembre
(diceeyembray)
December

Clothes and parts of the body

la camisa
(la cameesa)
shirt

la chaqueta
(la jacketa)
jacket

los pantalones
(los pantaloness)
trousers

los pantalones cortos
(los pantaloness cortos)
shorts

el calcetín
(el calsetin)
sock

la nariz
(la nareess)
nose

el ojo
(el o-ho)
eye

la cabeza
(la cabbeza)
head

el pelo
(el pello)
hair

la boca
(la bocca)
mouth

el cuello
(el cweyo)
neck

el hombro
(el ombro)
shoulder

el brazo
(el bratho)
arm

la mano
(la manno)
hand

el tobillo
(el tobeeyo)
ankle

la oreja
(la orreha)
ear

el mentón
(el menton)
chin

el dedo
(el deddo)
finger

la blusa
(la bloosa)
blouse

la muñeca
(la munyeka)
wrist

la falda
(la falda)
skirt

el codo
(el codo)
elbow

la rodilla
(la roddeeya)
knee

la pierna
(la peeyerna)
leg

el vestido
(el besteedo)
dress

el abrigo
(el abreego)
coat

el pie
(el peeyay)
foot

el dedo del pie
(el deddo del peeyay)
toe

el pulóver
(el pullover)
pullover

el zapato
(el zapato)
shoe

Colours and numbers

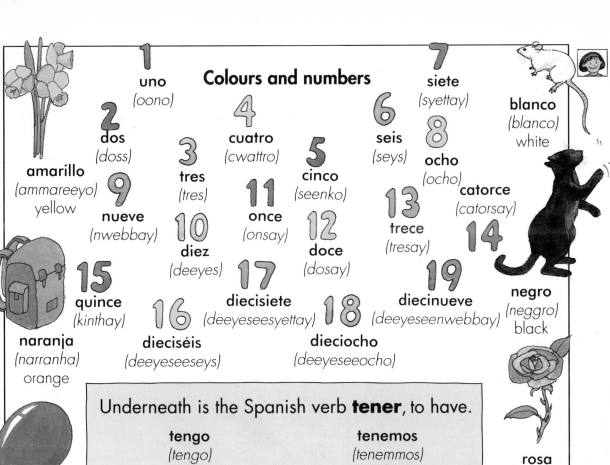

1 uno *(oono)*

2 dos *(doss)*

3 tres *(tres)*

4 cuatro *(cwattro)*

5 cinco *(seenko)*

6 seis *(seys)*

7 siete *(syettay)*

8 ocho *(ocho)*

9 nueve *(nwebbay)*

10 diez *(deeyes)*

11 once *(onsay)*

12 doce *(dosay)*

13 trece *(tresay)*

14 catorce *(catorsay)*

15 quince *(kinthay)*

16 dieciséis *(deeyeseeseys)*

17 diecisiete *(deeyeseesyettay)*

18 dieciocho *(deeyeseeocho)*

19 diecinueve *(deeyeseenwebbay)*

amarillo *(ammareeyo)* yellow

blanco *(blanco)* white

negro *(neggro)* black

naranja *(narranha)* orange

rojo *(ro-ho)* red

rosa *(rossa)* pink

Underneath is the Spanish verb **tener**, to have.

tengo *(tengo)* I have

tenemos *(tenemmos)* we have

tienes *(teeyennes)* you have (familiar singular)

tenéis *(tennayiss)* you have (familiar plural)

tiene *(teeyennay)* you have (polite singular) he/she/it has

tienen *(teeyennen)* you have (polite plural) they have

---

gris *(greess)* gray

verde *(berday)* green

20 veinte *(beyntay)*

21 veintiuno *(beynteeoono)*

22 veintidós *(beynteedoss)*

30 treinta *(treynta)*

40 cuarenta *(cwarenta)*

50 cincuenta *(sinkwenta)*

60 sesenta *(sessenta)*

70 setenta *(setenta)*

80 ochenta *(ochenta)*

90 noventa *(nobbenta)*

azul *(azool)* blue

100 cien *(seeyen)*

1,000 mil *(meel)*

1,000,000 un millón *(oon meeyon)*

marrón *(marron)* brown

31

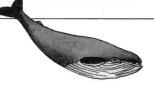

el cocodrilo
(el cocodreelo)
crocodile

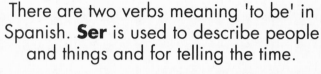

Animals

la ballena
(la bayena)
whale

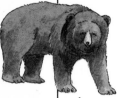

el oso
(el osso)
bear

el lobo
(el lobo)
wolf

There are two verbs meaning 'to be' in Spanish. **Ser** is used to describe people and things and for telling the time.

soy
(soy)
I am

somos
(somoss)
we are

eres
(erress)
you are (familiar singular)

sois
(soyis)
you are (familiar plural)

es
(ess)
you are (polite singular)
he/she/it is

son
(son)
you are (polite plural)
they are

la panda
(la panda)
panda

el delfín
(el delfeen)
dolphin

Estar is used to say where people and things are (eg 'She is in the dining room.'). It is also used to describe something that will not last long (eg 'It is snowing.').

la cebra
(sebra)
zebra

estoy
(estoy)
I am

estamos
(estammos)
we are

estás
(estas)
you are (familiar singular)

estáis
(estayiss)
you are (familiar plural)

el tigre
(el tigray)
tiger

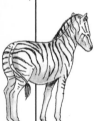

la gorila
(la goreela)
gorilla

está
(esta)
you are (polite singular)
he/she/it is

están
(estan)
you are (polite plural)
they are

el león
(el layon)
lion

el canguro
(el kangooroo)
kangaroo

el elefante
(el elefantay)
elephant

la jirafa
(la heeraffa)
giraffe

1/09 (40) 8/08

7/10 (47) 2/10

8/14 (63) 7/14